Animals I Like to Feed

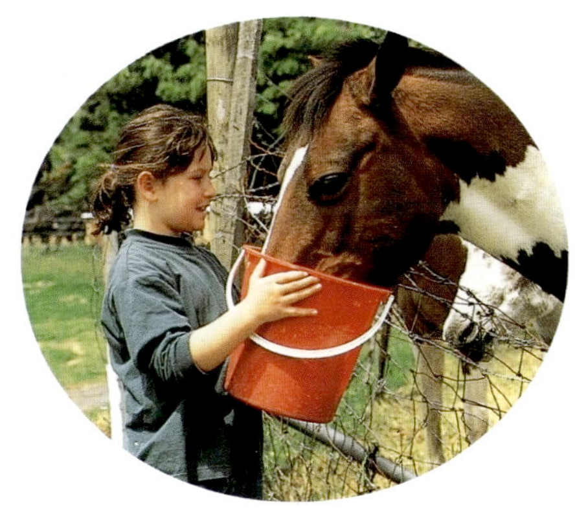

PETER SLOAN &
SHERYL SLOAN

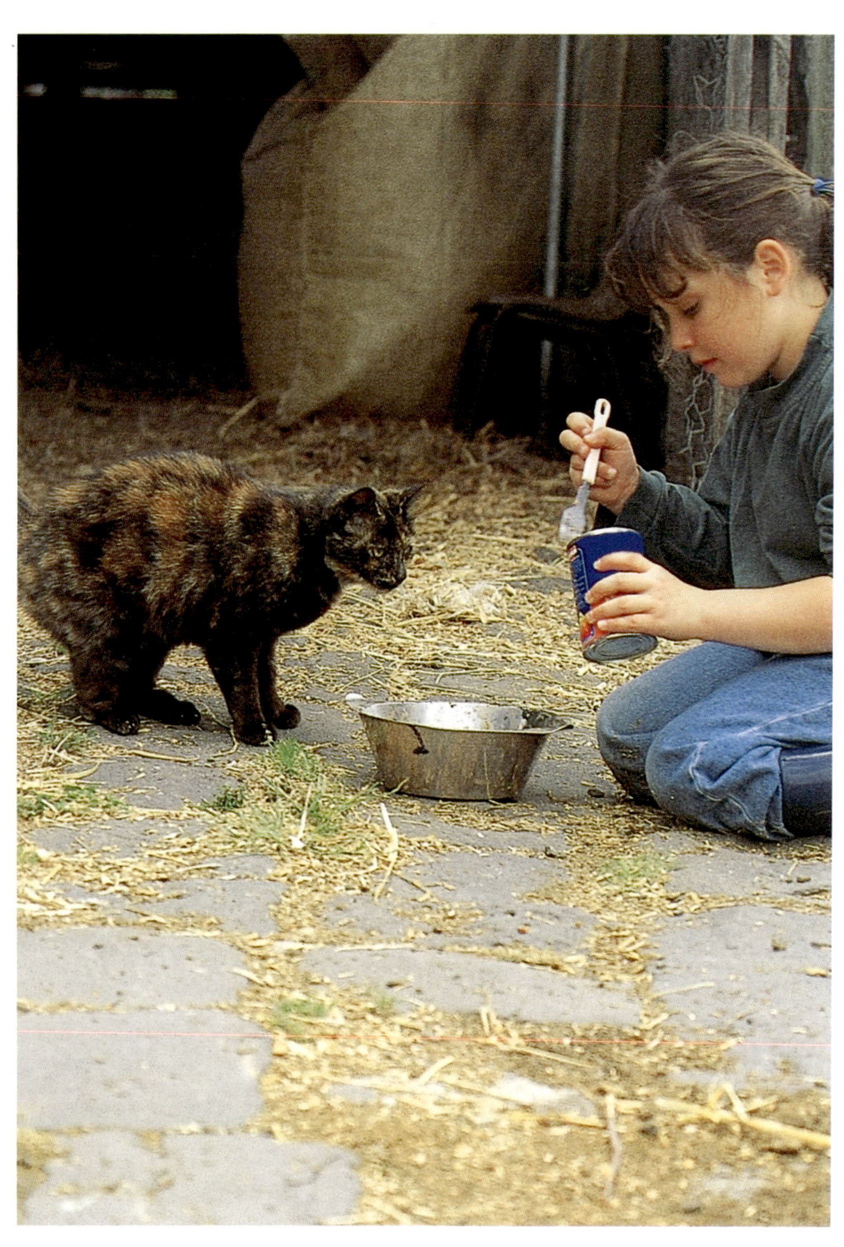

I like to feed cats.

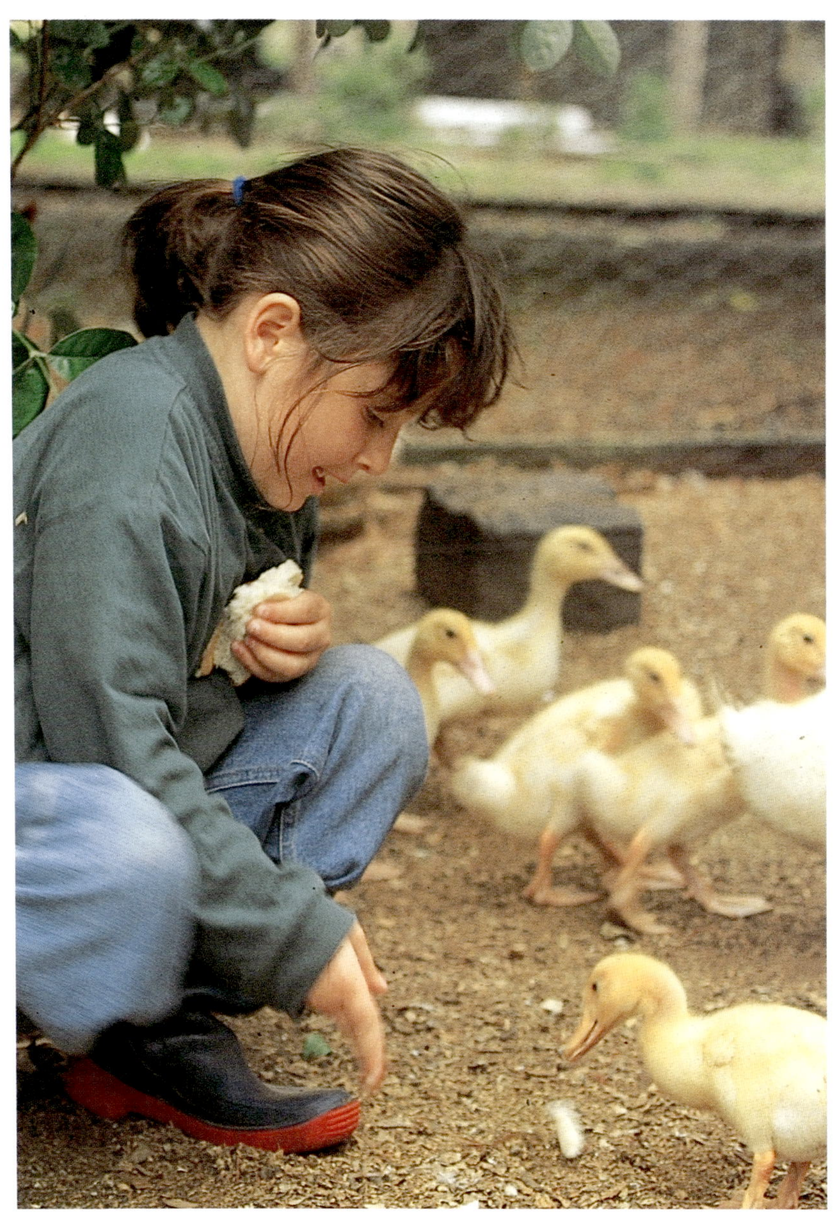

I like to feed ducks.

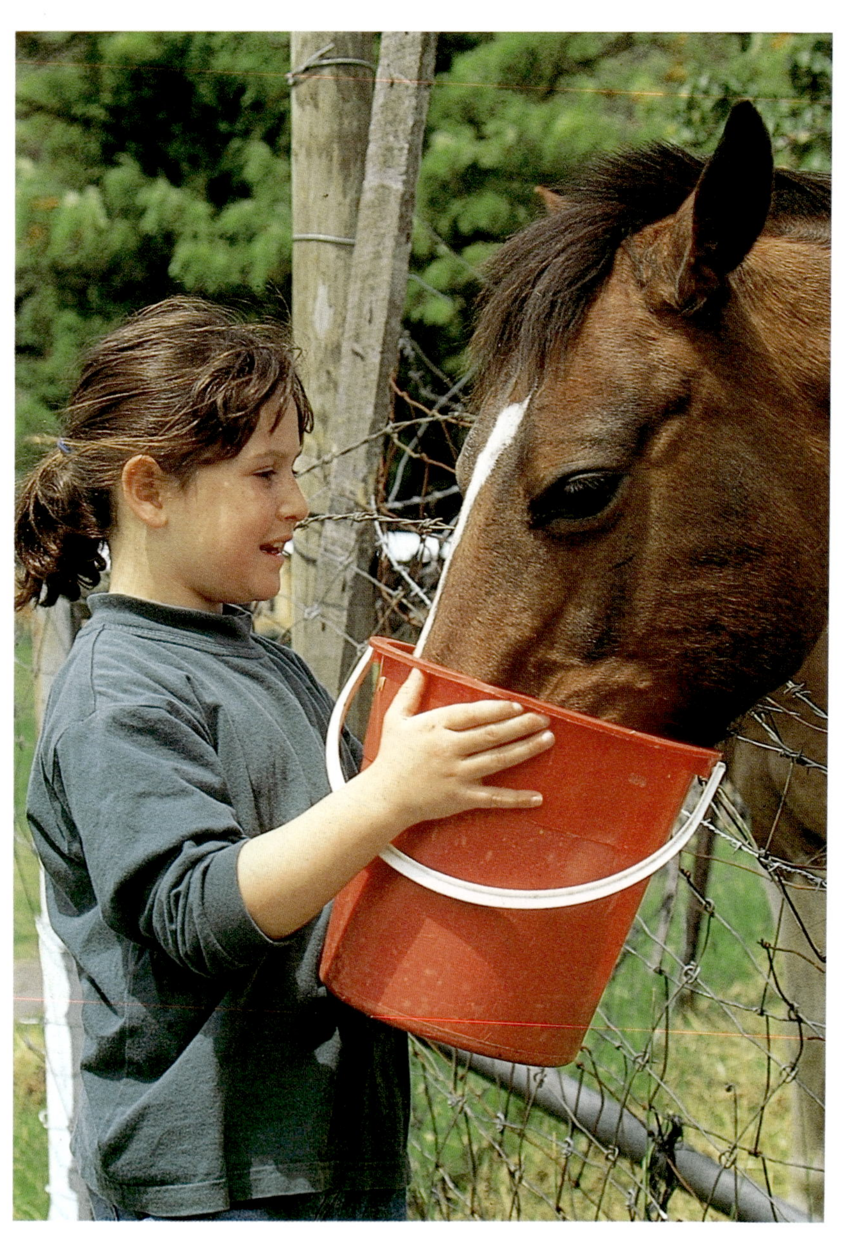

I like to feed horses.

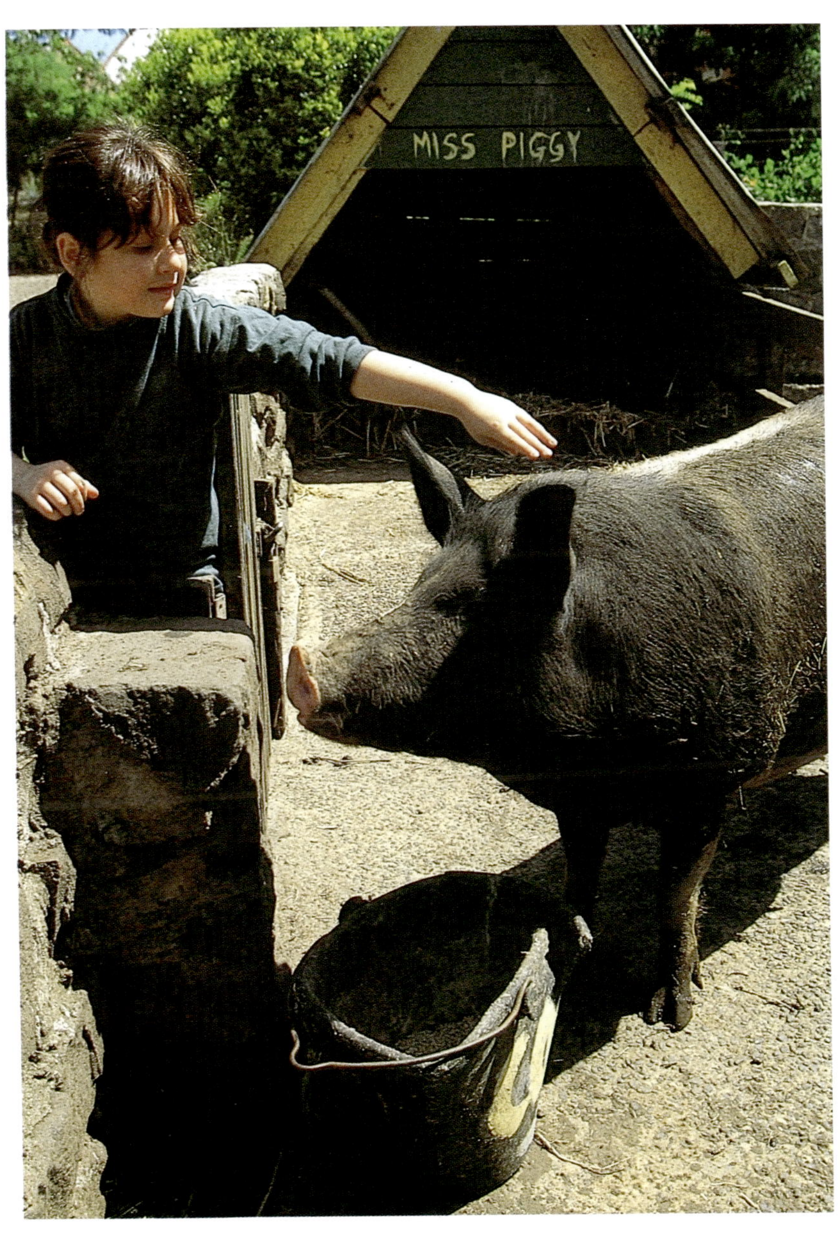

I like to feed pigs.

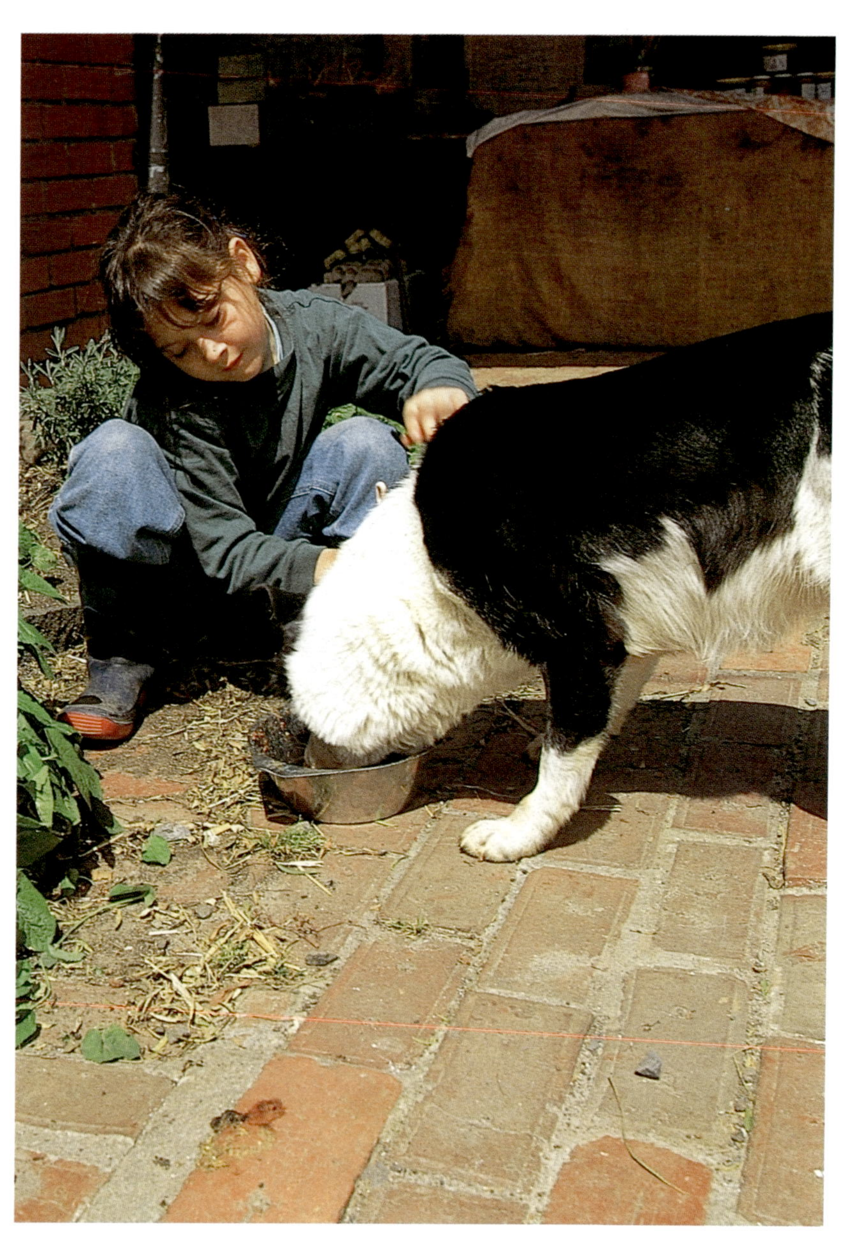

I like to feed dogs.

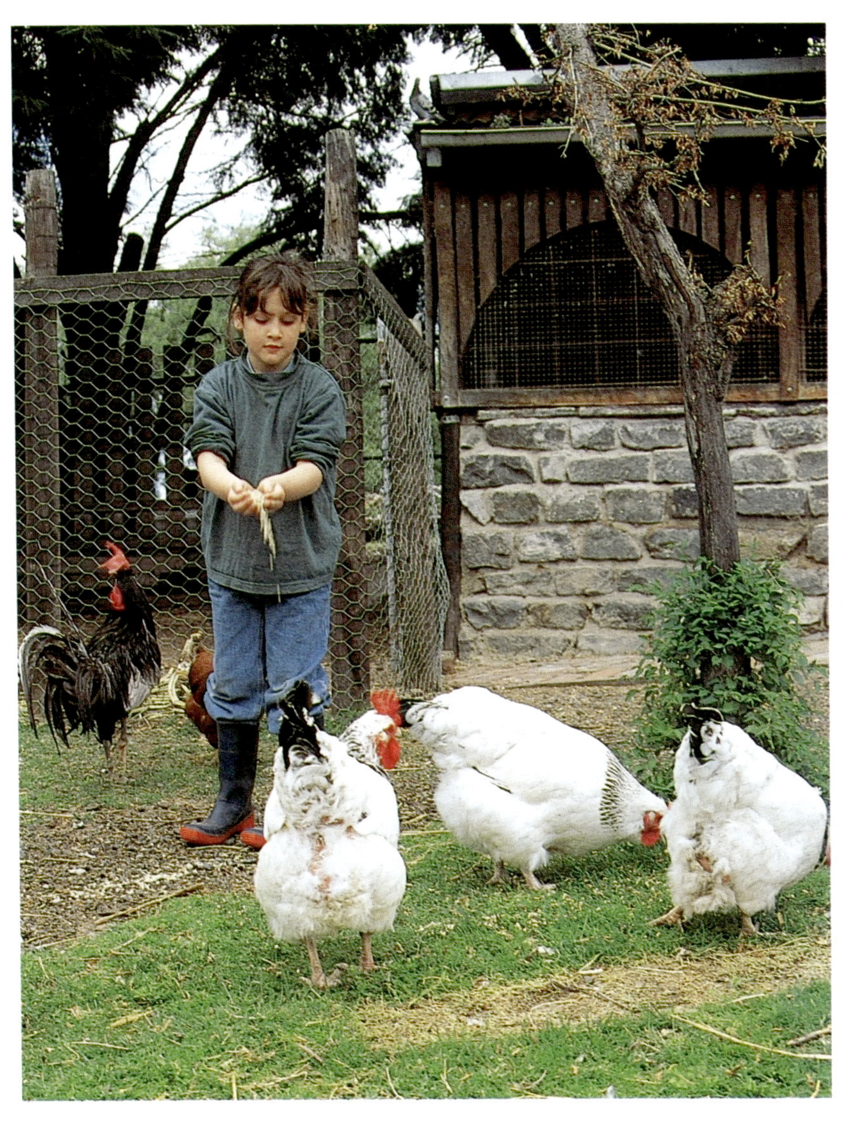

I like to feed chickens.

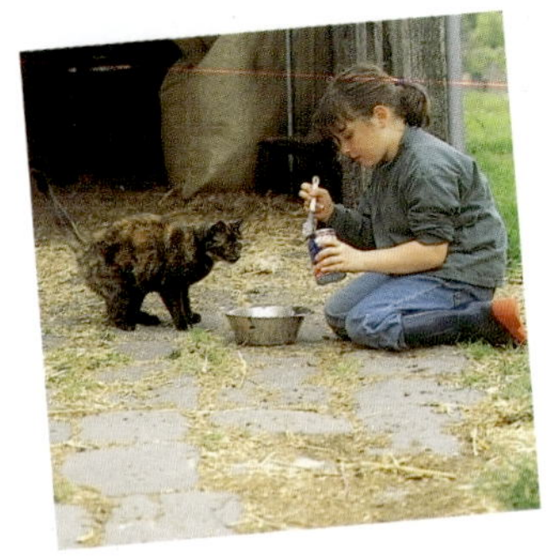

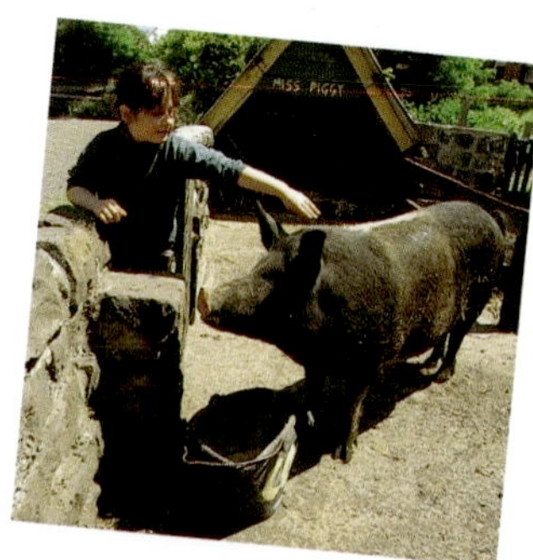

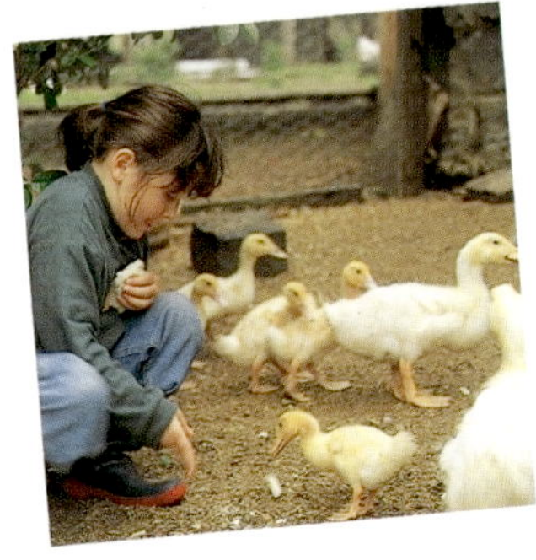

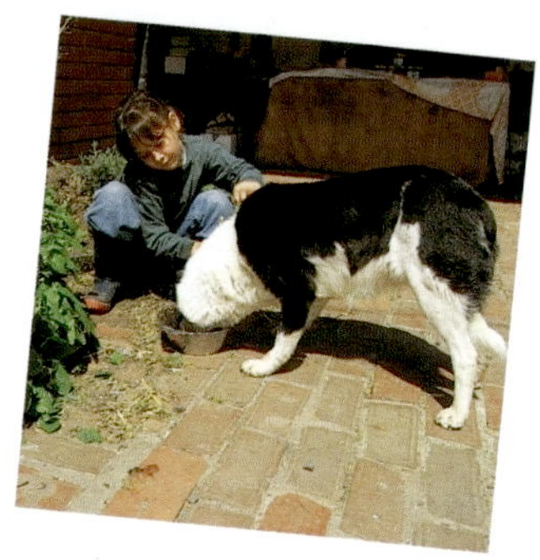

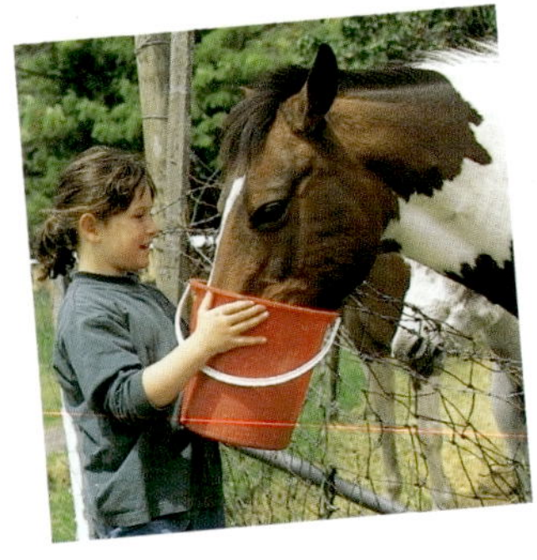

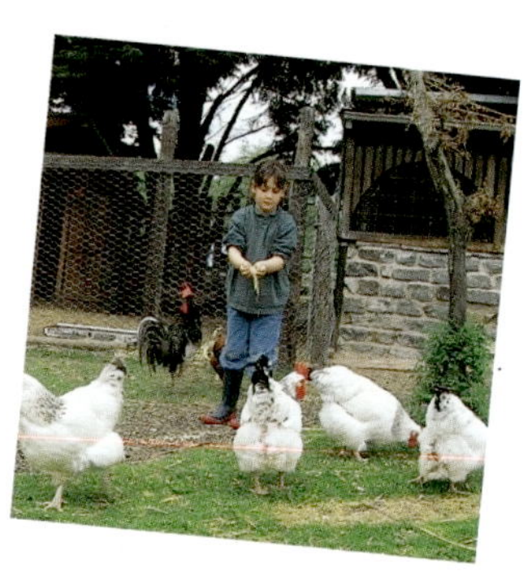

I like to feed
all of the animals.